SandCastle™

Primeros Sonidos

Ema y Eduardo

Cathy Camarena, M.Ed., and Gloria B. Ruff, M.Ed.

Consulting Editors

Lourdes Flores-Hanson, M.S.E., and Gloria Rosso-White

ABDO Publishing Company

capstone

www.capstoneclassroom.com

Credits
Curriculum Coordinator: Nancy Tuminelly
Cover and Interior Design and Production: Mighty Media
Child Photography: Steven Wewerka, Wewerka Photography
Photo Credits: AbleStock, Comstock, Photodisc

ISBN 978-1-4966-0329-6 (paperback)

Printed in the United States of America
873

SandCastle™ books are created by a professional team of educators, reading specialists, and content developers around five essential components that include phonemic awareness, phonics, vocabulary, text comprehension, and fluency. All books are written, reviewed, and leveled for guided and early intervention reading, and designed for use in shared, guided, and independent reading and writing activities to support a balanced approach to literacy instruction.

SandCastle Level: Beginning

Ee

ABCChDEFGH

IJKLLLMNÑOP

QRSTUVWXYZ

abcchdefgh

ijklllmnñop

qrstuvwxyz

Ema

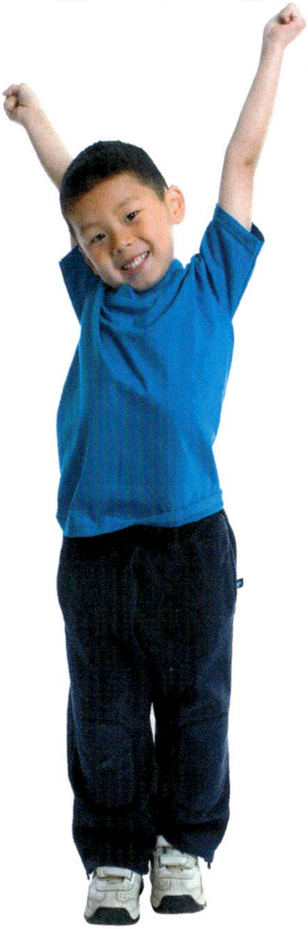

Eduardo

estufa

escoba

elefante

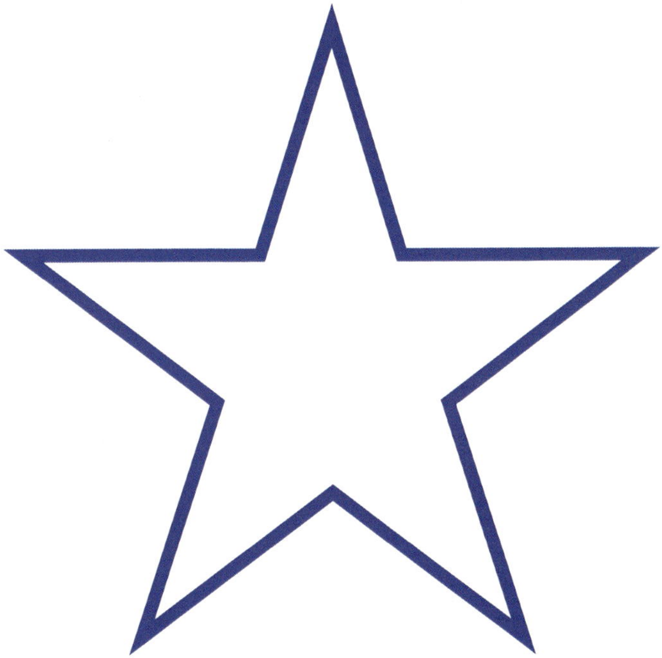

estrella

este

Mira la  .

Esta es una  .

El  es grande.

Mira la 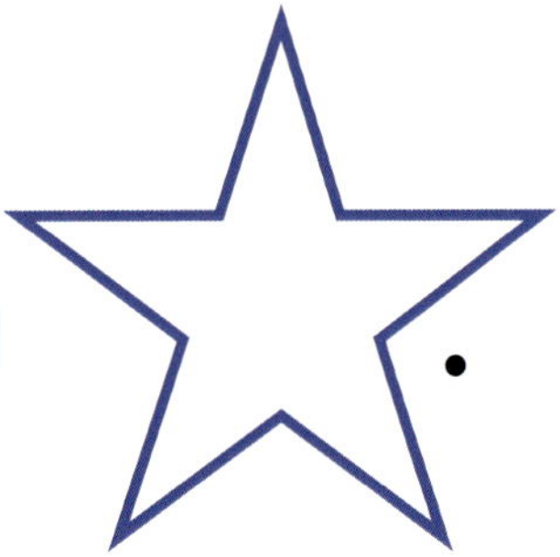.

Mira hacia el 

.

Ema tiene una estrella.

La estrella es roja.

Eduardo ve un elefante.

El elefante es grande.

Le ponen una
estrella al elefante.

Al elefante le gusta
la estrella.

¿Cuáles de estas cosas comienzan con e?

Más palabras que comienzan con e

edificio

embudo

enchufe

ensalada

escuela

About SandCastle™

A professional team of educators, reading specialists, and content developers created the SandCastle™ series to support young readers as they develop reading skills and strategies and increase their general knowledge. The SandCastle™ series has four levels that correspond to early literacy development in young children. The levels are provided to help teachers and parents select the appropriate books for young readers.

Emerging Readers
(no flags)

Beginning Readers
(1 flag)

Transitional Readers
(2 flags)

Fluent Readers
(3 flags)

These levels are meant only as a guide. All levels are subject to change.

www.abdopub.com

www.capstoneclassroom.com